Become a Master of Self-Control

with the kids of Camp MakeBelieve ™

Author:
Pamela M. Goldberg, RN, M.S.
Marriage & Family Therapist

Illustrator: Jimmy Boring

Creative Assistant: Elizabeth Arthur

Cover Design: 1grafixgirl.com

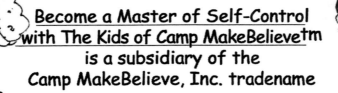

Become a Master of Self-Control
with The Kids of Camp MakeBelievetm
is a subsidiary of the
Camp MakeBelieve, Inc. tradename

1stBooks – rev. 8/31/01

READ WHAT EXPERTS ARE SAYING ABOUT
BECOME A MASTER OF SELF CONTROL
WITH THE KIDS OF CAMP MAKEBELIEVE

"Nothing in this world guarantees that your teens will turn out to be good people. However, if you are having behavioral problems with your child at a young age, the problems will grow in proportion to the child. Reading this book now, when your child is younger, will turn out to be one of the smartest things that a parent can do. Don't be surprised if several years from now, your child thanks you for buying this book."
Barbara Cooke, MS, editor and publisher, The ParentTeen Connection

"My 8 year old son has been going to Camp MakeBelieve for 3 years. He loves it and begs to go each new session. He handles his emotions better than anyone else in the family. He has gained a sense of self-esteem and sensitivity through Camp MakeBelieve."
Roberta Brown, Mom

"These stories about children's behaviors and problems are concrete and easy to identify with. The workbook activities and discussion points are excellent. This is just what is needed to help children learn to be successful!"
Adrienne Cox, Assistant Director, Dept. Family & Youth Services

"A great collection of common childhood behavior problems that both kids and parents can relate to. I commend Ms. Goldberg on her ability to relate to a variety of kids on their level."
Dr. Debra Barney, Child Psychiatrist

Junior Experts:

"I love the stories we read in Camp MakeBelieve. They help me learn when I have feelings what I can do about them. Each character has a different feeling inside of them that I get to learn about and learn how to fix them."
Eric Wilson, 7 years old

"I never knew how manipulating worked before until Miss Pam read me the story about Mattie the Manipulator. I like Camp MakeBelieve because I can help people out when they have bad feelings."
Brandon Brown, 9 years old

"I love when Miss Pam reads the Camp MakeBelieve stories and then we talk about the kids' problems afterwards. I learned to respect your friends and your parents and do what you are asked to do and to make the right choices."
Chris Arthur, 10 years old

"I like the stories Miss Pam reads to us because I learn not to be bad and that Camp MakeBelieve will make me happier. At the end of each story all the kids are happy. I like Camp MakeBelieve because we get to explain our problems and figure out how to use our words."
Courtney Thompson, 7 years old

Become a Master of Self-Control

with the kids of Camp MakeBelieve ™

About the Book

Camp MakeBelieve is an actual group program that has helped numerous children ages five through ten learn how to relax, become more motivated, confident, happy, and best of all; learn to become "Masters of Self-Control."

"Become a Master of Self-Control with The Kids of Camp MakeBelieve" relates three different stories about true-to-life characters growing up in today's rapidly changing society. Having been inspired by the Camp MakeBelieve counseling program, the characters face real-life situations that influence their social-lives, families and self-esteem as they find some real-life solutions. These stories should be read to a child at home with a parent or to a group of children in a learning or counseling environment. Because the stories are just the right length to hold a child's attention, the child will still have the focus needed to discuss the characters' problems and how they may relate to their own situations.

Each story ends with several innovative workbook activities that are practiced during the Camp MakeBelieve Program. Through art, clay sculpting, card games, acting, storytelling, meditation and fantasy; they are designed to help children learn how to manage their behavior and express their emotions appropriately, as well as to help them develop empathy and find solutions to the everyday problems that affect their lives.

The "Parent's Corner" gives parents many creative tips, suggestions and strategies that are used in child therapy sessions to help them reinforce the skills their children have learned in the workbooks, as well as examines their own feelings about their parenting practices. It also teaches parents insightful, creative and useful skills to better deal with a challenging child. Parents are encouraged to set limits and to use reasonable discipline that will empower their children to manage their own moods and behavior.

This book is highly recommended for parents, educators and mental health professionals who need a more creative, user-friendly resource to foster self-esteem and social skills in children between the ages of five and ten.

Children and adults alike will be delightedly amused with the emotional journeys of Mad Melly, Crazy Colby and Mattie the Manipulator. And with the help from the Kids of Camp MakeBelieve, the children in your life will become much happier, more confident and "Masters of Self-Control."

Table of Contents

Section I

Mad Melly Masters her Feelings
-Open Discussion (Q & A Period)..............1
....18
Workbook & Activities:
-A World of Feelings......................19
-Face Your Feelings.......................20
-Feel the Colors..........................21
-Why I Feel the Way I Do..................22
-Target Your Emotions.....................23
-Special Symbols..........................24
-Mini Mobile..............................25
-Crazy Animal Action Games................26
-Furry Feelings...........................27
-Get Yourself Connected...................28
-My Mood Thermometer......................29

Section II

Mattie the Manipulator Learns Fairness. 31
-Open Discussion (Q & A Period)...........54
Workbook & Activities:
-What Part of NO Don´t You Understand?.....55
-Attitude Counts..........................56
-Did You Say No?..........................57
-Express Yourself.........................58
-My Insides Caught the Lie................59
-Fair/Unfair Card Game....................60
-It´s OK To Manipulate Clay...............61
-Lying Makes Me Feel......................62
-Are You Sunny or Stormy?.................63
-The Power of Words.......................64
-Anti-Manipulation Slogan.................65

Section III

Crazy Colby Calms Down.
-Open Discussion (Q & A Period)...........67
....85
Workbook & Activities:
-Don´t Get Yourself Erased................87
-No More Bad Choices......................88
-He´s Got Nasty Habits....................89
-What Was I Thinking?.....................90
-Remember Your ABC´s.
    Always Be in Control..................91
-Master of Self-Control Card Game.........93
-A New & Improved You.....................95
-Imagine..................................96
-Who Needs Rules Anyway?..................97
-That´s the Breaks........................98
-I´m in Control!!.........................99
-My Fabulous Name........................100

Section IV

The Parents Corner.....................101
-Parenting Tips...........................104
    (Supplies Needed for Workbook Activities)
-Emergency Attitude Switch for You
    (E.A.S.Y.)............................106
-Imagine That!............................108
-Mood Changer Tips for Kids...............110
-Quality, Unique, Imaginative, Creativity
    for Kids (Q.U.I.C.K.).................111
-Master of Self-Control Achievement Certificate
....113
....115
About the Author.
    About the Illustrator,
    About the Special Assistant...........117

Acknowledgments

There are so many people in my life who have helped me along the way to make this book into a reality. First and foremost, I would like to thank my parents, for encouraging me to be *somebody*. Next, I would like to thank my husband and children for their endless support, and endless creativity.

I cannot thank enough my big brother, Ken Grossman, for helping to make this abstract concept a reality. Through his relentless guidance and support, Ken has helped make this book a very professional piece of work.

I would also like to thank my special assistant and very special niece, Liz Arthur, for her creativity, and dedication to this project. Without her ability to keep me in control, nothing would have ever been accomplished.

I would also like to thank my graduate professor, Pat Markos, for introducing me to the world of creative art therapy. Next, I would like to thank my internship supervisor, Andrea Krueger, for trusting in me and allowing me to practice these wonderful creative interventions in the many groups under her watchful eye.

To all the Kids of Camp MakeBelieve – thanks for your inspiration and for being such unique and incredible individuals!

Disclaimer

The ideas in this book come directly from the Camp MakeBelieve program. In this book, children will learn the difference between inappropriate and appropriate behavior.

The author and publisher are not responsible for any actions taken by any person/s who lead and/or participate in any of the games or activities in this book.

As in all situations, the children who participate in these activities should be calm and relaxed to insure that the child is focused and ready to learn new appropriate behaviors.

Have fun and I hope that Melly, Colby and Mattie entertain and teach you and your child!

Mad Melly
Masters Her Feelings

A Camp MakeBelieve ™
Story

About the Story

Mad Melly Masters Her Feelings is the first story in <u>**Become a Master of Self-Control with The Kids of Camp MakeBelieve**</u> series. Mad Melly is a little girl who only knows how to express one feeling and that feeling is anger. Melly's older sister, Lizzie, describes different scenarios where problems arise and Melly reacts with a very negative attitude. Melly doesn't seem to care about how her anger outbursts effect the people in her life. She also fails to notice that her friends stay far away from her when she gets into her "moods". Melly gets help in a local program in her home town called Camp MakeBelieve, where she learns to identify a wide variety of feelings, and to express her feelings appropriatley. Included at the end of this story is the workbook called "A World of Feelings". These activities are geared toward children ages 5 through 10 and can be done individually, or with the help of a parent, teacher or counselor.

Hi, I would like to introduce you to my sister Melly. Melly is her nickname. Her real name is Melanie. I love Melly very much, but sometimes she just pushes my love away. It seems that everything I say or do makes Melly very angry. I almost wonder if Melly was born with a problem where she can only feel one single feeling. Come on, let's read on, and I'll explain.

Remember I said that Melly only shows one feeling. It is really weird because when I get sad about something, I cry. When Melly gets sad, she turns angry. Let me explain. My sister Melly and I had a pet canary bird we named Ida. Melly played with Ida whenever she was home. She would let Ida out of her cage so Ida could fly around the house. It was really cool because when Melly wanted Ida to go back to her cage, all she would have to do is whistle, and Ida would fly from wherever she was and land right on Melly's finger. Melly was really attached to Ida.

One day Melly and I came home from school and found Ida dead in her cage. I got very upset and sad and started crying. Not Melly, she turned into a monster! She screamed, "Who killed my bird while I was at school?" She ranted and raged and turned her room upside down. Our mother came running to her room to see what all the commotion was about. She tried calming Melly down, but Melly would not let anyone near her. She stayed mad for a long time. That turned out OK because Melly was then grounded to her room for the next week and had plenty of time to be by herself and clean up her mess.

Then there was the day our family had the coolest birthday party for Melly. Our parents went to a lot of trouble trying to surprise my sister. My mom told Melly we were all going to the park to take a nature hike. We brought our water bottles, put on our hats, sunglasses and lots of sun screen. Melly was really excited because she loved going on hikes.

Boy did Melly's mood change fast when we drove up to the park. We started getting out of the car when a bunch of our friends and family ran up to us and yelled, "Surprise!" Melly looked really confused and froze in her seat. We all thought Melly would be so excited and happy to have a surprise birthday party. Not our Melly. She pouted and would not get out of the car. She was mad because she couldn't go on the nature hike.

Mad Melly Masters Her Feelings

Did I tell you yet about the time Melly got caught cheating at school? She didn't have time to finish her homework, so she asked her friend if she could copy off her assignment. Guess what happened? Her teacher, Ms. Sedgeworth, saw her copying and took the homework right out of Melly's hand. Miss Sedgeworth had a very mean look on her face and said, "It is against our school policy to cheat!"

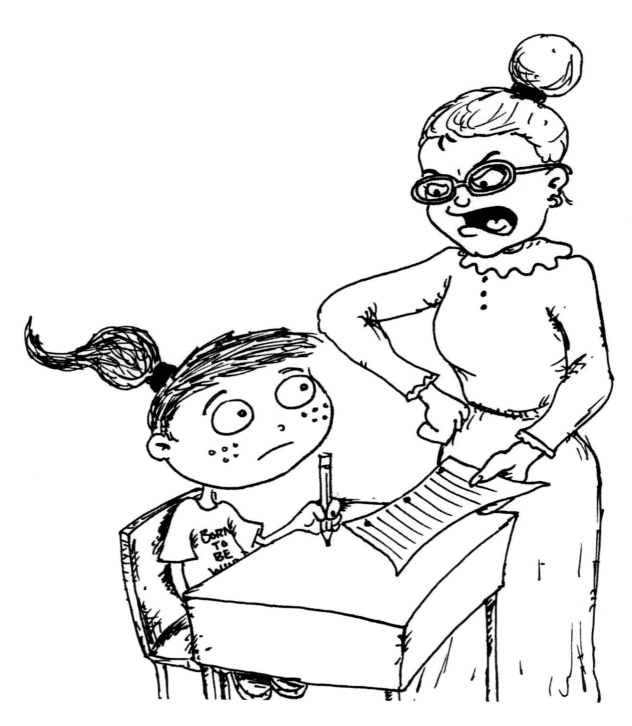

I would have felt so ashamed and apologized immediately. Not my sister. She got very red in the face, puffed her chest out and told the teacher in a very angry voice, "*Cindy told me I can copy, so there is nothing wrong with that!*" Well, Ms. Sedgeworth dragged her down to the principal's office and said, "*No student will have an attitude like that in my classroom!*" Boy did Melly get in trouble when she got home from school!

Mad Melly Masters Her Feelings

    I was with Melly the time that our mom was very sick with the flu. Poor Mom couldn't get out of bed for 3 whole days! I tried really hard to help Mom while she was sick. I heated her up soup and brought her soda to drink and tried to make her comfortable. Melly and I were home on winter break on one of the days Mom was sick. Dad just left for the office, and I was taking a shower. Mom said to Melly, "Please honey, go to the kitchen and get me the bottle of aspirin and water that is next to the sink." Melly was playing with her video game in Mom's room and said, "Not now Mom, ask Lizzie, I am just too busy."

Mom then got up and walked to the kitchen by herself. I found her leaning against the wall about to pass out. I helped her back to bed and took care of her myself. I then found Melly in the playroom. I said to Melly, "That was wrong of you Melly. You should have helped Mom. She almost fainted trying to get that medicine herself." I was trying to make Melly feel guilty so she would help out next time. Melly just looked at me and said, *"I was right in the middle of my video game. You weren't doing anything. Why couldn't you help Mom out?"* She got so mad that she wouldn't play with me for the rest of the week.

Mad Melly Masters Her Feelings

This is my sister Melly. I really don't understand her a lot of the time. I try to love her, but boy does she make it hard sometimes. She is just so angry all the time! Her friends just stay away from her when she gets in her bad moods. I can't stay away because I am her sister and have to live with her. Plus she is younger than me and I am supposed to keep an eye on her. I talked to my parents about Melly and they did not know what to do.

That was when I got the idea to talk to my school counselor, Mr. Junie.   Mr. Junie told me, "Not to worry Lizzie, lots of kids have a problem expressing their feelings properly, especially anger. You are lucky because you are getting help for Melly while she is still young." Mr. Junie really understood how confused we were about Melly's problem and that our family needed help.

Mad Melly Masters Her Feelings

Mr. Junie told me about a program in our town called Camp MakeBelieve. Mr. Junie said Camp MakeBelieve is a safe place where children have fun while learning about feelings. A small group of kids get together with this really cool counselor and have discussions about the problems that are affecting kid's lives. Stuff like bullies, teasing, attitude problems, peer pressure, family problems, and self-esteem.

The next day, I brought my parents to school to meet with Mr. Junie. Mr. Junie highly recommended that Melly attend the Camp MakeBelieve program. He also said that Camp MakeBelieve is a good place for all children to learn how to talk about their problems and behave appropriately. Guess what? My parents were so excited about Camp MakeBelieve that they signed Melly and I both up. Can you believe it?

Well, the next month Melly and I started going to Camp MakeBelieve. I was kind of nervous, and it goes without saying that Melly was pretty mad that she was being forced to go. It was really cool because we quickly became friends with the other kids in the group and felt comfortable sharing our problems with them. After the first session Melly and I couldn't wait to go back.

Can you believe that after only 8 weeks of Camp MakeBelieve, Melly's attitude improved? She seemed to be so much more relaxed and happy. All of a sudden Melly seemed to be making better choices and feeling really good about herself. I actually think Melly was proud of herself because she was now in control of her feelings instead of letting her feelings control her. How cool is that?

The End

Looking for Answers? Well then, ask the right questions...........

Mad Melly Masters Her Feelings

1.) Melly showed a lot of anger when her bird died. What do you think Melly was TRULY feeling inside?

2.) For what reasons do you think Melly would be angry all the time?

3.) Do you have any problems with bullies at school and/or being teased? What are some ways in which you can deal with them?

4.) Do you know anyone that gets angry a lot? Why do you think they are this way? What are some things that YOU can do to try and help them calm down?

5.) Do you remember a time when you were angry? Why were you angry?

6.) What are some things you can do to help control your anger?

7.) Sometimes things just don't work out the way we would like them to, but that is just a part of life that we all must accept. Do you remember a time when something didn't work out for you? How did it make you feel? What did you do to make yourself feel better?

8.) How do you think other people around you may feel when you get angry?

9.) How do you feel when someone gets angry with you?

10.) Instead of being angry with someone and yelling or having a temper tantrum, what kinds of things can you think of to show or tell that person how you are feeling?

A World Of Feelings
Workbook

Dear Kids,

I hope you enjoyed reading my *Mad Melly Masters Her Feelings* story in <u>Become a Master of Self-Control with The Kids of Camp MakeBelieve</u>. Boy did Melly have a hard time figuring out how she was feeling! She never stopped to think about anything. She just let herself go straight to anger. If you see yourself as having a problem expressing your feelings, you are not alone. Melly is like many of the kids in my *Camp MakeBelieve* program. During *Camp MakeBelieve*, I have helped hundreds of kids sort out their feelings and find solutions to their problems.

When you do these workbook activities, you will learn not only the vocabulary for a "world of feelings", but also you will learn lots of creative ways to express yourself. When you express yourself the right way, you don't hurt anybody, and you start to feel better yourself. Kids are able to do most of these activities alone, but please, ask someone to join you if you need help. Feel free to e-mail me at pam@campmakebelieve.com if you have any questions or concerns about the story or the workbook activities. Have fun and remember, there are a "world of feelings" out there so don't be afraid to feel them.

Thanks,

Pam Goldberg

FACE YOUR FEELINGS

Below are many different feelings that kids experience. We have already drawn in what the facial expression might look like. Go ahead and color the hair and accessories. Be creative. Hang the chart in your room. When you can't figure out what you are feeling, look at your chart and see if you can find the right feeling.

sad

happy

scared

playful

proud

mad

jealous

confident

confused

pretty

disappointed

mean

energetic

loved

aggressive

tired

Feel the Colors

It is amazing how different colors can remind us of a certain feeling. Below are 10 feelings. Next to each feeling, write down the name of the color that the feeling reminds you of. Write the word with the color crayon of the feeling. For example, use the color red crayon to write the word red.

happy _____

sad _____

angry _____

lost _____

disappointed _____

proud _____

frustrated _____

loved _____

bored _____

scared _____

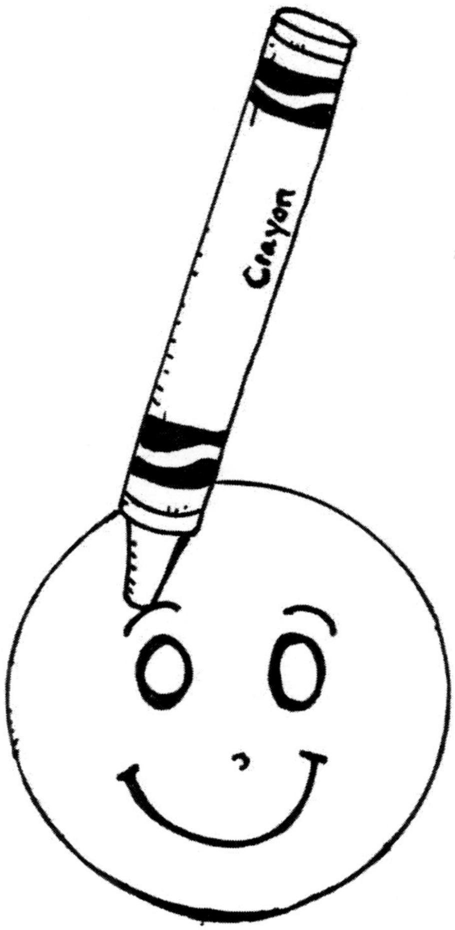

Why I Feel The Way I Do

Feelings are often brought on by something that happens. Under each feeling word, write down three things that could happen to make you have that feeling. For example, under "Happy" you may have this feeling because it is a beautiful day outside.

MAD

1._____

2._____

3._____

HAPPY

1._____

2._____

3._____

PLAYFUL

1._____

2._____

3._____

ASHAMED

1._____

2._____

3._____

SAD

1._____

2._____

3._____

FRUSTRATED

1._____

2._____

3._____

 **Target your EMOTIONS**

In the space below, make circles inside of circles like a dart board. Starting with the middle circle color in each circle the color you think the emotion would be. Put your favorite emotions toward the middle and work your way to the outside with the yuckiest emotions toward the outside. Make sure the color of the circle is how the feeling feels to you. Make an arrow pointing from the word to the circle.

Proud

Excited

Scared

Confident

Frustrated

Lonely

Disappointed

Embarrassed

Happy

Sad

Angry

Focused

Stressed

Make this into a poster size board and then hang your emotions target in your room. When you are feeling bad, stand about 8 feet from your target. Throw a ball of socks or a koosh ball to the middle feelings in your target. When you hit the middle feelings 6 times in a row, take a break and see if your mood is improved. If not, start over until you are feeling better. Have fun and don't knock over anything.

 # Special SYMBOLS

Symbols are signs that everybody understands no matter what language they speak. For example, the symbol of a heart usually means love. Make your own special symbol next to the feeling below. Cut out the cards. Make a game out of your own "language". You can write down the symbol and have people guess how you are feeling.

HAPPY	CALM
ANGRY	PLAYFUL
HUNGRY	HURT
FRUSTRATED	COLD
AGGRESSIVE	DISAPPOINTED

Mini-Mobile

Illustrated below are 8 different faces. Fill in and decorate the faces with different feelings. Be creative.
Put string through the punch out holes and hang above a doorway or a mirror.

Crazy Animal Actions Game

Below are 10 cards with an animal and how that animal is feeling. Cut out the cards. Put them in a stack, face down. By yourself or with a friend, pick up one card at a time and pretend you are that animal having that feeling.

Disappointed Dragon	Hyper Hyena
Frustrated Porcupine	Lonely Lion
Angry Gorilla	Ashamed Puppy
Gentle Giraffe	Happy Horse
Sad Kitten	Frightened Mouse

Furry Feelings

OK, so kids sometimes have a really hard time saying what they are feeling like. Here's an idea.
When someone asks you how you are feeling, tell them what animal you feel like. Below are 10
different feelings that kids have. Fill in the first blank for the animal a kid could be feeling like
and the second blank write down why you feel like that animal. The first one is done as an example.
Happy is the feeling - puppy is the animal – play and have fun is why you are feeling like that animal.

Happy: I feel like a _____puppy_____ because _____all I want to_____
      do is play and have fun_____ .

Sleepy: I feel like a _____ because _____
_____ .

Playful: I feel like a _____ because _____
_____ .

Hungry: I feel like a _____ because _____
_____ .

Confident: I feel like a _____ because _____
_____ .

Loved: I feel like a _____ because _____
_____ .

Ferocious: I feel like a _____ because _____
_____ .

Tired: I feel like a _____ because _____
_____ .

Hyper: I feel like a _____ because _____
_____ .

Silly: I feel like a _____ because _____
_____ .

Get Yourself Connected

Here are some feeling words. Connect each feeling word with the character on the right who looks like he/she could be having that feeling.

Nervous

Confident

Embarrassed

Hopeful

Surprised

Stressed-out

Angry

Confused

Jealous

Sad

Happy

MY MOOD THERMOMETER

Our moods are like thermometers. They go from 0 to 100 in a few seconds. We can start out in a happy mood, and then something happens to bother us and WHAMMO! we get angry. Let's take a look at how our moods change. Here are some feeling words. First circle ten of the feelings that you have, then line then up in order with the mildest on the bottom and the yuckiest on the top. Next to each feeling, color in 10 degrees of the thermometer that you think the mood reminds you of.

calm   Hyper   aggressive   embarrassed   lonely   **frustrated**
bored   angry   **confused**   NERVOUS   ANNOYED   happy   Sad
scared   ENRAGED   Jealous   tired   SURPRISED   Confident   ashamed

Mattie the Manipulator Learns Fairness

A Camp MakeBelieve ™
Story

About the Story

    Mattie the Manipulator Learns Fairness is the second story in the **Become a Master of Self-Control with The Kids of Camp MakeBelieve** book. Mattie is an endearing little girl from a newly divorced family who has learned the art of manipulation to get her own way. Mattie does not understand the meaning of the word "no". Through tears, tantrums, begging, whining and cuddling, Mattie has learned she has the skills to convince her dad, grandma, teachers and friends into giving her whatever her heart desires. Mattie's parents are torn because they both feel so guilty that the family has broken up. Included at the end of this story is the workbook called "What Part of *NO* Don't You Understand?" The goals of these workbook activities are to help children understand fairness, honesty, empathy and self-control. These workbook activities are geared toward children ages 5 through 10 and can be done individually, or with the help of a parent, teacher or counselor.

Hello, my name is Madeline which I think sounds way too girlie, so I have everyone call me Mattie. I'm 9 years old. I have two little sisters named Clara and Breanne, a dog named Zirgo and two cats named Alf and Murray.

My life was pretty normal until I turned 6 years old, and my parents got a divorce. I hated it so much I used to cry all the time, but now I am pretty used to it. My sisters and I have to spend half of every week with Dad and then the other half of the week with our mom. It gets us so mixed up all the time because we leave things at one house and forget to bring stuff to school or to the other house. I guess it gives my parents something to fight about or otherwise they probably wouldn't be talking at all. I'm glad you're reading my story because boy, do I have some things to tell you!

Like I said, my parents got a divorce when I was 6 years old.   That was a long time ago, but I remember it all like it was yesterday.   It was awful!   My mom cried all the time. My dad just honked the horn for us to come outside, and we were all confused.   Mom and Dad yelled at each other all the time for the dumbest stuff! Boy, would that make my sisters and I feel bad!

As time went on, we got used to going to Dad's new house and then back home to Mom's again. Actually, it turned out to be kind of fun because Dad NEVER asks us to do any chores like Mom does. Dad takes us to totally cool places like the movies, the circus and to ball games. Dad never really yells at us, or makes us do time-outs, or even take a shower. Can you believe he doesn't even smell our breath to make sure we brushed our teeth? It's incredible! There are no rules at Dad's house!

It is really strange because Dad didn't seem this nice when he was living with us. When he lived with us, he was constantly yelling at us to pick up our back packs, hang up our coats and stuff like that. Actually, he yelled at us about everything. After he moved into his own house, he sort of gave up on rules. This is when I started learning a few interesting things to get my way. Read on, and you'll see what I mean!

When I am with my dad on his visits, I feel like I really have it made. He takes us to the store to pick out what we want to eat when we stay at his house. One day Dad told Clara to go pick out the cereal, and she picked out Apple Jacks. I started pouting because she got to pick out the cereal. My dad said, "Mattie, what's wrong honey?" I said, "Clara ALWAYS gets to pick out the cereal, Mom ALWAYS lets Clara have her way!" Clara right away said, "Daddy, that's not true, Mommy picks it out, and she makes us eat cornflakes!"

Dad looked very uncomfortable, and I felt like this was my moment to get what I wanted. "Dad, I have an idea." I said with a smile, "We could all pick out our own cereal and that would solve the problem! That's a great idea, don't you think?" My sisters were jumping up and down thinking it was the greatest idea I ever came up with.

Dad said, "Mattie, I don't know. I think we should just buy one box of cereal." You know what I did then? I can't even believe it myself! I started crying. Right there in the store! Great big buckets of tears were rolling down my face. Through my tears I looked over at my little sisters who were smiling because they knew I was tricking Dad. It seemed like a long minute, and then Dad said, "Okay, fine, you guys, go and pick out your own box of cereal."

Right then (it was magic I tell you), my tears went away. I had a big ole' smile on my face, and off I ran to get a box of Sugar Smacks! OH, MAN! This was a dream come true! All three of us got to have our own box of cereal! I was on to something. I could feel it in my bones. I felt like "SUPER MATTIE", ready to get anything I wanted.

Mattie the Manipulator Learns Fairness

    After the divorce when we visited over at Grandma's house, we learned a few tricks there too. Grandma felt so bad about the divorce that she would do anything for my sisters and I. She always fell for the big, sad, puppy eyes that I would give her when I wanted something. I would say, in my ever-sweet Mattie-way, "Please Grandma, please Grandma. Mom and Dad NEVER let us do anything fun." Believe it or not, she always gave in. It was the easiest to trick her when she was busy cooking, knitting, or watching television. We knew that when Grandma was busy, she didn't want to be bothered with us, so she gave in.

For some reason this strategy did not work so easy with Mom. When she saw my sisters and I whine, cry, have tantrums and make demands, she would get very annoyed. Mom never has a problem making us do things that we don't want to do. Stuff like clean our rooms and eat vegetables. BLAH! Mom always makes us do homework and go to bed at 8:00 on school nights. Mom still makes us do everything the same as before the divorce, and she gets so cranky all the time when we don't do it. Mom always sticks to her "no's". She always says, "What part of 'no' don't you understand?" It was useless to argue with her.

43

When we tried talking Mom into doing something that she really didn't want to do, she would get angry and yell at us and make us go to our rooms. Then of course if she was with us when we tried tricking our dad or our grandma, Mom would say, "Tell them NO! Can't you see they are manipulating you?" Of course, Mom was always the meanie because she always stuck to her decisions, and Dad was the hero when he caved in and let us do what we wanted. I started to feel bad for Mom when this happened because I knew I was wrong, but then, what the heck? I was getting my own way and loving it! Boy, life was confusing, and I wasn't sure how I should act.

For my 9th birthday, things started to backfire on me. My mom bought me a shiny new pink bike with white streamers off the handlebars and a pretty white seat. It was just the kind of bike I always wanted. I hugged and kissed her and ran off to ride my bike. After telling her she's the greatest, of course! I am always very thankful when I get a cool present. Of course, if it's not what I want, I pout. But I'm sure you already figured that one out about me.

The next day, Dad came to pick us up to celebrate my birthday again. He took me, my sisters and his new girlfriend, Debbie, to my favorite Italian restaurant. Dad gave me lots of dopey clothes (that Debbie probably picked out) and girlie jewelry. UGH! I sat there and put on my *I didn't get my way and now I'm going to make everyone miserable face*. Dad gave a big sigh and said, "Honey, what would you like the most for your birthday?"

My mind started working fast, and I perked right up. I put the sweetest smile on my face and I told him, "Oh Daddy, I would looooove a new video system for my room!" You know what he did next? He took us to the mall and bought me exactly the kind I wanted. I gave him a hug and of course told him he was the greatest. My dad and Debbie sure had a big fight about me changing my presents and she started acting different to me. Life sure was confusing when I was 9!

Even though I had all this cool stuff, I started feeling really sad all the time. Adults were always annoyed with me, and everyone was starting to think that I was getting very spoiled. My friends thought I was a temper-tantrum baby. I started getting into the habit of whining with my friends and storming out of their house when they wouldn't play what I wanted to play. What they didn't realize was that this had turned into a game for me. I never heard the word "no". I kept after people until I wore them down. My teachers were getting sick of me, and my poor mom was so angry and frustrated all the time.

A couple of months after my 9th birthday, my teacher called my parents in for a conference at my school. Mom and Dad were in the classroom talking to my teacher while I waited outside in the hallway. When they finished talking and opened the door, I could tell they were both very angry. I tried running up to my dad and snuggling up to him. He ignored me. I then started crying and hugged on tight to my mom. She undid my hands from her waist and started walking to the car.

Dad followed us home. When we got there, my parents sat me down and said, "Mattie, your teacher says that you are very manipulating to her and the other students to try to get your way. Is this true?" Manipulating? What kind of word is that? I didn't even know how to say it, spell it, or explain it. How could I tell them if it was true? They explained that a manipulator is someone who doesn't take "no" for an answer, lies and throws temper tantrums to get her own way.

I knew I was caught, so I thought up a story real quick to stay out of trouble. "Mooooom, Daaaaad, my teacher hates me. That's why she told you that!" I went on and on about how my teacher doesn't listen to me. I said, "She never lets me do things the other kids get to do, and she makes me stay in at recess time when the other kids get to go outside. She is so mean, and she is such a liar!" I guess I went too far this time because for once, my parents didn't believe me. I think they already knew that I was a master at manipulation but they didn't realize how my "game" was causing problems at school and with my friends.

Mattie the Manipulator Learns Fairness

My teacher knew how my behavior was causing me problems and told my mom and dad about a program in town called Camp MakeBelieve. Camp MakeBelieve is a place where children meet and talk about how important it is to always tell the truth and be fair. Even if this means you are going to get into trouble or not get your own way. I learned that people don't like being lied to or tricked into doing things they don't want to do. In Camp MakeBelieve, I made art projects and wrote stories to use my imagination. I was able to manipulate people in my stories but not in real life anymore.

Camp MakeBelieve also had a class for parents called *The Parent's Corner*. My mom and dad took a "time-out" where they learned how to discipline and set limits on us kids so we can't get away with stuff all the time. They found out it is important in every kid's life to have rules that everyone understands, routine that is easy to follow (like chores and stuff) and structure where the kids know what is expected of them. This should be the same in both houses when the parents are divorced. Camp MakeBelieve taught me and my family a lot. Isn't that cool?

The End

Looking for Answers? Well then, ask the right questions...........

Mattie the Manipulator Learns Fairness

1.) Do you know anyone that behaves like Mattie? How does it make you feel when they behave this way?

2.) Mattie's dad's girlfriend Debbie began to act differently towards her. How do you think Debbie felt about Mattie's behavior?

3.) Do you remember a time when you had lied to get your own way or to hide something from someone? How do you think that person may have felt once they discovered the truth?

4.) Do you remember a time when someone had lied to you? How did that make you feel once you found out the truth?

5.) Have you ever tried to trick someone into doing something they didn't want to do? Why? How do you think it made that person feel?

6.) What are some rules that you have in your house?

7.) Do you have an easy-to-follow daily routine (chores, etc) or responsibilities?

8.) What are some things that you know are expected of you from your parents (chores, truthfulness, kindness, etc.)? Teachers? Friends?

9.) Imagine a world where no one ever had any rules to obey or responsibilities to carry out. Imagine what it would be like if everyone could get their own way by manipulation (lying, whining, crying, etc.). What would this world be like? Would it be a happy or sad place? Why?

What Part of *No* Don't You Understand? Workbook

Dear Kids,

I am very excited that you read my *Mattie the Manipulator Learns Fairness* story from <u>Become a Master of Self-Control with The Kids of Camp MakeBelieve</u>. Mattie sure figured out how she can trick people so she can get her own way. I discovered from talking to hundreds of kids in my Camp MakeBelieve program that kids don't feel good when they are able to trick people. Kids have an amazing way of whining, crying, negotiating, and begging to get what they want. Then, the funny thing is, that "getting stuff" is not really what makes them happy.

You will be delighted to discover through doing these workbook activities that being honest and reponsible is what makes kids feel good about themselves. You will also discover that when your parents set limits on your behavior, you feel safe and cared for. Have fun doing these workbook activites. If you need help, ask a parent to do the activity with you. If you have any questions or concerns, feel free to send me an e-mail at pam@campmakebelieve.com. I look forward to hearing from you.

Thanks,

Pam Goldberg

ATTITUDE COUNTS

The attitude we have shows people how we are feeling. A good attitude shows people we are feeling good. With a good attitude, we smile, say nice things and do nice things.

In the space below draw yourself with a good attitude.

What are you doing? _____

What are you saying?_____

How do you feel?_____

Did You Say *NO?*

Mattie is a girl who won't take "No" for an answer. Draw a picture of a time you were able to talk someone into doing something you know they didn't want to do. Use the space below for your drawing.

Think about how the person felt who you tricked.

EXPRESS YOURSELF

Mattie the Manipulator sure liked to get her own way all the time. Let's find out how a person might feel when they don't get their way.

Activity

Think about a time when you did not get your way. Draw a picture in the space below that tells what happened. Write down how you felt.

MY INSIDES CAUGHT THE LIE

When a person tells a lie they sometimes feel bad or guilty. The words don't just come out of your mouth, but they stay inside your body too, making people feel strange. Some people get a sick belly, some maybe a headache, others just feel all icky inside because they know that what they told was not the truth.

Draw what you feel like on the inside when you tell a lie.

|  | # FAIR/UNFAIR CARD GAME |  |

Below are 15 cards with stuff that kids do or say listed on them. Cut out the cards, shuffle them, put them in a pile, words down. By yourself or with someone else, pick up one card at a time and talk about the behavior as being fair or unfair.

Your parent asks you to take out the trash.	Your mom asks you to help out cleaning up after dinner.	Your parents pick out the place you are going on your summer vacation.
Your teacher makes you sit out of recess for fighting.	You have to sit in the backseat while your brother or sister sits in front.	You forget your lunch and the kids in class chip in and give you food.
Mom wants you to take a vitamin everyday.	Your friend doesn't want you to have any friends but him.	Your teacher asks you to stay everyday after school to clean the class room.
Your mom wants you to stay home with your dad so she can go to the mall by herself.	Your parents want you to babysit your brother when you have a huge homework assignment due.	Your friend forgets his lunch and asks you to share yours.
You need to use the phone and your sister has been on it for an hour and won't hang up.	Your brother will not let you do your homework on the computer because he is always using it.	Mom asks you to watch your younger sister while she takes a nap.

IT'S OK TO MANIPULATE CLAY

Mattie was a Master of Manipulation. She could convince people to do things they really did not want to do. Get some clay and make a "Master of Manipulation" sculpture.

Remember! You are not getting graded on this. Have fun and make your sculpture as creative as you want.

Write or tell a story about your sculpture. What kind of creature is it? Where did it come from? How old is it? Is it a girl, a boy or a creature? What does it like to do for fun? What kind of attitude does it have? Does your creature have any bad habits? What kind of rules and consequences does this creature have? Give your story a happy ending by telling how your creature can change its behavior.

Give your sculpture a certificate for doing such a good job!

THIS AWARD IS PRESENTED TO:

_____

FOR MASTERING A GOOD ATTITUDE

PRESENTED BY:

_____

 # LYING MAKES ME FEEL...

Make-believe you are telling a lie so you can get your own way. Describe what you think happens when you tell a lie.

When I lie. . .

The shape I feel the most like is _____

The color I feel the most like when I lie is _____

The texture I feel the most like when I lie is _____

The animal I feel the most like when I lie is _____

When I get caught in a lie . . .

The shape I feel the most like is _____

The color I feel the most like when I get caught in a lie is _____

The texture I feel the most like when I get caught in a lie is _____

The animal I feel the most like when I get caught in a lie is _____

I imagine when I lie, other people feel. . .

The shape people feel the most like when I lie is _____

The color people feel the most like when I lie is _____

The texture people feel the most like when I lie is _____

The animal people feel the most like when I lie is _____

ARE YOU SUNNY OR STORMY?

Attitudes can be good or bad. When you trick someone, like Mattie would do, that is showing a stormy (or bad) attitude. Below is a list of behaviors that kids have that show if their attitude is sunny or stormy. Are you sunny or stormy? Draw a picture of a sun for a good attitude and a picture of a lightening bolt for a bad attitude next to the behavior listed below.

1. Tell someone you are sorry._____

2. Say mean things to one friend about another friend._____

3. Tell your mom you cleaned your room when you really didn't._____

4. Say good-morning to a kid walking past you in the hallway at school._____

5. Ask your dad if he would like help washing his car._____

6. Ignore your mom when she asks for help cleaning up after dinner._____

7. Start crying when your dad tells you he can't buy you a new toy right now._____.

8. Take turns choosing the game you are going to play._____

9. Ask Mom if she would like some help getting dinner ready._____

10. Beg your teacher to let you play outside after she has told you no._____

THE POWER OF WORDS

Mattie would cry, beg, whine and pout when she couldn't get her own way. She really wasn't expressing her feelings the right way. It is better for kids to figure out how they are feeling and then use the feeling word to express themselves. It is amazing that when you talk about how you are feeling, you suddenly begin to feel better because you understand why somebody is telling you "no". If you are told "no", you must accept the reason.

In the sentences below, fill in the blanks with how you might be feeling.

Dad, I feel _____ that you won't let me have a new toy.

Mom, I feel _____ when I have to clean my room and my brother doesn't have to clean his room.

When you yell at me I feel _____.

I left my homework at home and now I feel _____.

The kids at school made fun of me because I forgot my lunch. It made me feel _____.

I need to work harder on my math and spelling words and that makes me feel _____.

When I can't play outside because I didn't do my chores, I feel

_____.

Mom, I feel _____ when you ask me to take a shower when I'm watching my favorite television program.

Dad, I feel _____ when you promise me something we are going to do, and then you don't have time to do it.

ANTI-MANIPULATION SLOGAN

Now that you have learned that it is wrong to manipulate people, be active in letting other people know too!   Be president of your own club.

IT'S OK TO NOT GET YOUR OWN WAY!

IT'S OK TO NOT GET YOUR OWN WAY

Some suggestions: Make your own banner and buttons with the slogan listed above. Hang them in the house and pass them out to your friends. Be creative! Go ahead and draw a picture of yourself on the inside of the slogan with a PROUD expression on your face. Hurray for you! You did it!

Crazy Colby Calms Down

A Camp MakeBelieve ™ Story

About the Story

Crazy Colby Calms Down is the third story in **Become a Master of Self-Control with The Kids of Camp MakeBelieve** book. Colby is a delightful little boy with a very happy attitude who gets into constant trouble because of his poor impulse control. Colby never thinks before he acts and winds up doing the dumbest things. Colby takes us on an adventure through his trouble at school, his boy scout camp-out and his neighborhood shenanigans. Colby always winds up with horrific consequences for his reckless behavior. It takes him burning down his tree fort before the local fireman suggests help through the Camp MakeBelieve program. Included at the end of this story is the workbook called "Don't Get Yourself Erased". These workbook activities are geared toward children ages 5 through 10 and can be done individually, or with the help of a parent, teacher or counselor. The goals of these workbook activities are to teach children the difference between thoughts and feelings, how to think before they act, respect rules, enforce consequences for breaking rules and learn relaxation techniques so that they calm down.

Hi, my name is Colby, but everyone calls me Crazy Colby. They call me that because sometimes I do the craziest things, and I don't even know why. I try not to act crazy all the time, but sometimes I just can't help it. Sometimes being as crazy as I am is OK, but other times it just gets me into trouble.

Crazy Colby Calms Down

One of the places where I always seem to be getting into trouble is at school. Most of my teachers like me, but they say that I talk way too much and that is my biggest problem. During the first month of school, I spent more time trying to talk to my friends while my teacher, Mrs. Byrd, was trying to teach the class. Boy did that turn out to be a big mistake! Can you believe she put my desk facing the wall so I wouldn't be distracted during class time?

Every morning she gives me a fresh start sitting with the rest of the class, and low and behold by first recess my privilege is over! Mrs. Byrd gives me the hand signal that I know so well. I have to get up and move my desk all by myself to the far corner of the room where I can't distract the other kids! Can you imagine the humiliation? Not only is this totally embarrassing, but it is soooo boring being away from the other kids! Not to mention the fact that Mrs. Byrd gets quite impatient with me.

Crazy Colby Calms Down

Wait till I tell you what happened during field day! Field day is a really fun day because the whole school gets to play fun games like tug-o-war and have relay races. Field day was my favorite day of the whole year. This year on field day I was so excited that I just couldn't control myself. I was fidgeting in my seat, tapping my pencil on the desk and making little "clicking" sounds with my tongue. Mrs. Byrd warned me that if I couldn't calm down, I wouldn't be able to participate in field day. We had only thirty minutes to go before we got to go outside and boy did I feel hyper! Mrs. Byrd passed out graham crackers and milk. I tried really hard to stay in control and stop being so crazy, but you won't believe what happened next!

My friend Tommy passed gas, and we both started laughing really hard and I just couldn't stop. My eyes were watering. I started snorting, and the milk started squirting right out of my nose! It was so funny! I tried all my strategies of staying in control. I bit the insides of my cheeks. I took three deep breaths. I pictured Mrs. Byrd giving me time out, but nothing seemed to work. I do believe the last straw for Mrs. Byrd was when I rolled off my chair and fell onto the floor. I laughed myself right into trouble. I guess you can figure out that there was no field day for me.

Crazy Colby Calms Down

Mom says I'm so *impulsive* all of the time. Big people are always telling me that I'm impulsive. Mom told me this means I don't think about the consequences of my behavior before I do things. I really don't know what she's talking about! I mean, of course I think about things I'm going to do. I am always thinking about all the cool things I'm going to do later. Things like what video games I'm going to play or who I'm going to play with after school. Isn't that what she's talking about?

Mom signed me up for Boy Scouts because she thought it would make me responsible. I loved my new group of friends! They thought I was *so* funny every time I clowned around. I really felt important because I got so much attention. But wouldn't you know, I started taking up all the attention trying to make people laugh. The scout leader was constantly stopping what he was doing to tell me to be quiet and pay attention. I knew the scout leader was getting very tired of correcting me and probably wished I never signed up for his group.

Crazy Colby Calms Down

My scouting adventures only lasted till the first camp-out. I told myself that I was going to behave and not get into any trouble. On the first night as we were all roasting marshmallows in the camp fire, I was distracted by the loud croaking of toads. WOW do I love toads! I quickly decided to go and start a collection of toads to bring home to my yard. I tossed aside my marshmallow stick and ran into the main tent where the utensils were kept to find a container for my new collection. Then I went on a hunt to gather the best bunch of big, beautiful, croaking toads.

Well, I didn't want my toads to get cold or lonely so I put them in the sleeping bags of my fellow scouts for safety. I didn't think they would mind. I mean, who doesn't just *love* toads? I must have forgotten to tell them because that night when we were all sleeping, kids all over the place were screaming and crying. I was shouting for them to all **stop it** because they were **just toads,** and they won't hurt you.

Crazy Colby Calms Down

That was when the scout leader took me aside. I tried explaining to him that I just wanted the kids to keep the toads warm until I could bring them home. He looked very disgusted with me. I felt very confused and guilty. I thought I was doing the right thing, but once again I didn't think through the consequences. I wasn't surprised in the morning when the scout leader woke me up early, and I saw my mom's station wagon at the campgrounds. I was going home. I wasn't allowed back in scouts after that.

My troubles at school were not the only reason people called me "Crazy Colby". My nickname actually started because of my pranks in the neighborhood. My friends and I do lots of cool stuff after school. We play video games, build tree forts, ride bikes and do pretty much anything you can think of.

One day I found a packet of matches and got all of my friends to watch while I burned them in the tree house. We **knew** we weren't supposed to play with matches because it is **very, very dangerous**. For a while my friends thought it was really cool to watch the matches burn until a fire started in our tree fort. I will tell you that fire started getting bigger and bigger, and we started running.

Crazy Colby Calms Down

I ran all the way home and right upstairs to my room. My mom knew something was wrong but when she asked me if everything was OK, I said, "Yeah Mom, sure." A few minutes later, we heard sirens getting close to our block. I was shaking so hard under the covers in my bed. My mom must have been suspicious because she came upstairs. When she saw me, I was as white as a sheet and about to throw up because I was so nervous. She was thinking I was sick and went to get a thermometer when the door bell rang.

HOLY MACKERAL! I was standing at the top of the stairs, and I almost passed out when I saw the fireman standing at our door.   I couldn't hear what they were saying, but I could tell by the sound of my mother's voice and the look on her face when she called me down the stairs that she was angry! "Colby, I've had it with you this time!", she said. Well, I'm sure you could figure out what happened next. I never got in so much trouble in my life. My punishment lasted forever it seemed, and the worse part was my friends were not allowed to play with me anymore. I felt so ashamed of my behavior and frustrated that I make such bad choices sometimes.

Crazy Colby Calms Down

My mom invited the fireman (his name was Bill I found out) inside for coffee to talk about my problem. The fireman told my mom about a program he heard of called Camp MakeBelieve. He said that Camp MakeBelieve is a program that kids can go to where they learn self-control and to get a grip on their bad habits. My mom looked up the Camp MakeBelieve web site on our computer and found out that it wasn't available in our town yet. She was really excited to find out that she could order a workbook that they actually use in the Camp MakeBelieve classes. My mom seemed really relieved that she was getting me some help for my problem.

By doing the Camp MakeBelieve workbook activities, I learned to think before I act, to be more responsible, and most of all to calm down. I got to do most of the activities by myself, but some of them were fun to do with my mom. I really started practicing what I learned from these activities at home and at school. Probably the best thing I learned is that it is cool to be crazy sometimes, but if I want to act crazy, it has to be in the appropriate place like a water park or zoo or somewhere like that. I should **never** act crazy when it is bothering someone else or can be dangerous to myself or to others.

Crazy Colby Calms Down

Things are getting better for me all the time. The nickname "Crazy Colby" has stuck with me, but I really am not that "crazy" anymore. Personally, if it were up to me, my nickname would be changed to "Calm Colby", but what can you do?

The End

Looking for Answers? Well then, ask the right questions...........

Crazy Colby Calms Down

1.) Colby was playing with matches in his tree house where he set it on fire. What are some other dangerous things you can think of not to do? What are some of the consequences of these things to consider?

2.) Can you remember a time when you did something before you thought out the consequences? What happened? How did you feel afterwards?

3.) Colby learned that there are certain times and places in which you can act silly. What kinds of places and times can you think of where it is more appropriate to act goofy?

4.) What are some things you can think of to do to help yourself think through your plans before carrying them out?

5.) Everyone in the world has rules that they must obey ... even the President and the Queen of England. What are some rules that you must obey at home? At school? In church? What kinds of consequences follow if you break any of those rules?

6.) Why do you think Colby's friends were not allowed to play with him any more?

7.) Can you remember a time when you had acted silly or did something when you weren't supposed to? What happened? What were the consequences of your behavior? How do you think the other person/people around you had felt about your behavior? What could you have done to prevent it from happening?

Don't Get Yourself Erased
Workbook

Hi Kids,

I hope you enjoyed reading my *Crazy Colby Calms Down* story in <u>Become a Master of Self-Control with The Kids of Camp MakeBelieve</u>. I sure enjoyed writing it. I realize that *all* kids act kind of crazy sometimes because kids are kids. But, when crazy behavior starts to get you into trouble and your friends stay away from you because they don't want to get into trouble, believe me, you have a problem. In my Camp MakeBelieve program, I have helped hundreds of kids figure out how they can get a grip on their behavior and feel good about themselves.

By doing the activities in the "Don't Get Yourself Erased" workbook, you will learn how your behavior affects other people and best of all, how you can become a "master of self-control". Most of these activities can be done by yourself. If you have difficulty with an activity or would have more fun doing it with another person by all means, ask someone to join in on the fun. If you have any questions or concerns about my story or the workbook activities send me an e-mail at pam@campmakebelieve.com. Have fun doing these activities, and enjoy being in charge of your behavior.

Thanks,

Pam Goldberg

Pam Goldberg

No More Bad Choices

On the left are behaviors that kids do or say that are bad choices. Write down next to the behavior what you think the consequences should be.

Behavior	Consequence
A boy hit a kid because he took his favorite ball to play with.	
A girl took roller blades from her friends garage without telling them.	
Someone told a rumor about a friend that wasn't true.	
You yelled at your sister because she accidently broke your yo-yo.	
Your brother ignored Mom when she asked him to take out the trash.	
You didn't come in the house when Dad told you it was time for dinner.	
You told your teacher that the dog ate your homework.	
A boy told his mom that he already finished his homework when he really didn't.	
A girl got caught throwing a ball around the house when she knew it was against the rules.	
A girl waited until the night before to read a book for the book report that is due in the morning.	
You didn't complete your chores and told your parents that you did.	

He's Got Nasty Habits

Make a clay sculpture of a monster with bad habits. Write or draw below what his bad habits are. How would his habits annoy you and other people around him?

WHAT WAS I THINKING?

Think back to a time when you were really out-of-control. Maybe you were having a tantrum, maybe you were fighting or maybe you couldn't stop arguing. In the space below, draw a picture of YOU being out-of-control. On the bottom of the page write about what you were thinking and how you were feeling.

I was feeling_____

I was thinking_____

How did I get so out-of-control? _____

Remember Your ABC's
"ALWAYS BE IN CONTROL"

Make a list for strategies to stay in control. Below are five strategies.
Try to list TEN more.

_____'s   strategy list for self-control
          (your name)

1. Count to 50

2. Take three deep breaths

3. Ignore or walk away

4. Draw a picture

5. Write in a journal

6.

7.

8.

9.

10.

11.

12.

13.

14.

15.

 **Master of Self-Control Card Game**

Below are 14 cards with situations on the front. On the back are two ways to respond. Pick the answer that shows are a "Master of Self-Control". Cut out the cards, put them in a stack and play with a friend or adult.

A kid cuts in front of you in the lunch line.	You are feeling very tired and hungry. You find your mom in the kitchen.
Your dad asks you to help rake the leaves and pull weeds in the yard.	Mom is carrying in big bags from the grocery store.
Your best friend asks you for your homework so he can copy it.	Your teacher assigned a challenging book report due in one week.
It's the day the big fair is in town. Your mom asks you to help do some things around the house before you go.	Your little sister just got into your favorite crayons and broke them all.
The puppy just chewed up your new shoes and your other shoes are not the ones you want to wear today.	Your brother just won an award at school for being Student of the Month. You haven't won it yet.
Your teacher asks you to be a friend to a new kid in school, but you want to go play with all your other friends.	You are at the store with your Dad and you really want an ice-cream cone, but dad says "Not today".
It's a school night and you have a regular bedtime. You want to stay up and watch a television show.	Mom just gave you a new chore to do around the house because she feels you are responsible enough to do it.

A. Tell mom you are starving and ask nicely for a snack. B. Run in the kitchen, open the fridge and drink from the juice container.	A. You elbow him and tell him to move. B. Ask him politely to please go to the back of the line.
A. Continue what you are doing and ignore mom. B. Immediately help mom with the groceries without being asked.	A. Tell your dad that you will just put on your coat and shoes and be right out to help. B. Tell him that you're too busy.
A. You cry and complain that it's too hard and it's not enough time. B. You get started right away reading the book. It's hard work but it's a challenge.	A. Tell him you're not allowed to cheat, so he can't have your homework. B. You say "Sure, here it is, but don't tell anybody."
A. You know she's little and shouldn't have left them out for her to get into. Calmly tell her it was wrong to do. B. Scream at her and yell at her to stay out of your stuff.	A. Cry and pout and refuse to help because you had plans. B. Help mom because the quicker you get it done, the quicker you get to go!
A. Pout any time someone says "congratulations" to your brother. B. Be happy for your brother, he deserves it and one day you will too!	A. Put on the old ones. It's just a little puppy teething! B. Yell at the dog, scream at your mom and cry.
A. Tell dad "That's not fair, I never get anything!" B. You say to dad, "That's OK Dad, I know we don't have time anyway."	A. Ask the new kid to play with you and your friends...you can never have enough friends! B. Play with the kid, but make the new kid feel bad that you have to.
A. Demand more allowance and stomp off to your room. B. Happily take the new chore, being more responsible is good!	A. Ask Mom to tape the show for you so you can watch it another time. B. Sneak to watch t.v. when Mom and Dad go to bed.

A NEW AND IMPROVED YOU!

Go back and look at your picture on the "What Was I Thinking" page. Now give it a better ending where you stay in control.

I am feeling_____

I am thinking_____

How did I stay in-control?_____

IMAGINE

Go to a quiet place where you can relax. Take 3 deep breaths.
Now, imagine you are floating in the sky on a big white fluffy
cloud. You feel very relaxed and very free. Notice in your mind
how blue the sky is, and how warm the sun feels on your skin.
Now, pretend that the cloud drops you off in a village with a huge
castle. Surrounded by the castle are little houses, animals and
people. You walk through the village and discover that you are the
ruler of this village. Everyone looks to you with respect. You
suddenly feel responsible and in complete control.

On the next page, use your imagination and draw your village. Give
this picture a title. Write down how you feel when you look at your
picture.

I feel _____ when I look at my picture.

Who Needs Rules Anyway?

If you were the Ruler of your own kingdom, what rules would you have? Write them down on the rules board below. Remember, all of the people in your kingdom will obey your rules!

Rules for My Kingdom

1.

2.

3.

4.

5.

6.

7.

8.

9.

10.

11.

12.

13.

14.

15.

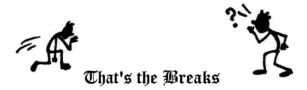

That's the Breaks

Now, if you were the Ruler of your own kingdom, you would also have consequences to go with your rules. Perhaps someone has broken one of your rules, what would the consequence be? Write them down on the board below. Everyone in your kingdom will have a consequence to go with bad behavior if they break a rule. Look at your "Who Needs Rules Anyway?" chart and write down the consequence for breaking that number rule.

Consequences for My Kingdom

1.

2.

3.

4.

5.

6.

7.

8.

9.

10.

11.

12.

13.

14.

15.

I'm In Control!

Draw a picture of yourself as a "Master of Self-Control"

What are your
in-control thoughts?

What are your
in-control words?

Where are your
hands, feet & body?

I am feeling _____

MY FABULOUS NAME

Write your name in BIG BLOCK FANCY LETTERS.   Put the letters long-ways. Next to each letter write something positive about yourself that starts with that letter. Have a parent help or look in a dictionary if you need extra suggestions.

Here is an example of my name:

Now, on the next page do your name!

Hang this in your room to remind yourself everyday that you are unique and special.   Don't forget to practice what you wrote!

The Parent's Corner

Dear Parents,

Raising three children of my own with Attention Deficit Hyperactivity Disorder, as well as dealing with hundreds of children in my Camp MakeBelieve program, I am very aware just how frustrating it is to deal with children's emotions on a daily basis. The characters in my Camp MakeBelieve stories are real life kids. They have tantrums, manipulate the heck out of their parents, and are so impulsive it makes your head spin. You have to love them though because those same personality traits that make us crazy are also the ones that make these children so endearing.

Children, as well as adults, must first learn to identify *how* they are feeling before they can learn to express themselves in an appropriate manner. Sounds easy, right? Sorry to say that if it were that easy there wouldn't be so much road rage, divorce, domestic violence and children being victimized at school. The good news is that when children are taught early on how to identify and express their feelings appropriately during calm situations, the better equipped they will be to handle their emotions when under stress or during peer pressure. By helping your child use these Camp MakeBelieve workbook activities, and with a little patience and guidance from you, your children will learn to express themselves better and live happy and healthy lives.

Parenting Tips

Supplies you will need for the workbook activities:

construction paper
scissors
markers, crayons, pencils
play dough or clay
poster board
quiet time and lots of imagination!

1. Hang up your child's "Feeling Faces" chart in an easily accessible place (kitchen, bedroom). If your child is having a difficult time expressing a feeling, bring them to the chart and have them point to the feeling they may be experiencing.

2. During a quiet time (on a road trip or at nap time), take your child through a simple meditation. Ask your child to lay back, close his eyes and take a few slow deep breaths. Then make up a story such as: imagine you are playing your favorite game with your favorite person. Ask them simple questions to encourage their imagination. Such as: "Where are you?", "Who are you with?". Be creative.

3. Always have drawing accessories available (construction paper, crayons, colored pencils). When your child gets in a "mood" have him/her draw a picture of what he is feeling. Use colors to express certain feelings. To prompt an angry child, say "Wow, I sure can tell you are mad. What color is mad to you? Can you show me on paper?" They may draw scribbles at first, but really get into talking about the scribble. As kids get older, their drawings get more complex. Don't be afraid to talk about the different characters in the drawings. Prompt them with "then what happened", or "tell me more".

4. Get your child into the habit of playing with molding clay or play dough. When in "a mood" have them make an object of what/who they are mad at, then smash the clay when done.

5. Remember - you are a role model for your children. Don't be so surprised if you whine, complain, yell or pout that your children copy your behavior. Set a good example always. If you do get out of control, apologize and explain you are working on your problem dealing with stress too.

6. Examine your own role as a parent. How do you feel when you say no to your child? Guilty? Mean? Powerful? Talk to your spouse about your roles as parents. Where did you get your parenting ideas from?

7. It is important to set limits for your child when they break the rules. Limit setting is best when done immediately (especially for small children), but, if you are angry, take a time out and wait until you have completely calmed down before you discipline your child. Think rationally about the consequence and let the punishment fit the crime. For example, if a child makes a mess, have him clean it up. If a child steals, have him pay back the person he stole it from.

8. Time-outs are a good time to cool off and think about the behavior. While in time-out, have your child draw a picture about the behavior that got him in trouble. After the time-out is finished, talk about the picture and give it a new and improved ending.

9. Hearing is believing! Tape record your child when they are screaming or having a tantrum. Let the child listen to it and discuss how the situation could be different next time. Go ahead and tape yourself and your spouse during an argument. How do you sound?

10. Talk to your child about what *you* do to control your anger/stress/frustration. Make yourself a list along with your child from the Melly Anger List activity. Hang your list up and use these strategies to change your negative feelings into more positive and productive feelings.

11. Have fun with your kids! Play games, go bike riding, watch their activities, sing songs, dance, be crazy. Try to keep the house quiet one hour before bedtime.

12. Display the Emergency Attitude Switch for You (E.A.S.Y.) page included in the Parent's Corner. Together you and your child can figure out what emotional state he is in and then have strategies ready to change his mood.

13. Display the Mood Changer Tips for Kids workbook activity (in Parent's Corner) on the refrigerator and have your child practice different techniques to get out of a bad mood.

14. Discuss the stories of Mad Melly, Mattie the Manipulator and Crazy Colby immediately after reading them to your child. Ask your child questions to prompt a discussion about the story.

Emergency Attitude Switch for You
is
E.A.S.Y.

Attitudes are like light switches, they turn on or off like the flick of a switch. The attitude *switch* is hidden deep inside your brain. "Things" happen, and all of a sudden you are in a yucky, dark place. Thank heavens children have the power to turn their yucky switch off and turn their bright light on! Learn how these E.A.S.Y. strategies will work to help you and your child be more relaxed, happy and in-control. Below are seven different attitudes that kids get into. Under each attitude are emergency things that you can do to help switch your child's light to the bright, happy place you want to be. With your child first identify what mood they are in, then help him to do the exercises listed under that mood.

I. <u>The Whiner</u>

1. Draw a picture of what the problem is.
2. Find new solutions for your problem.
3. Practice asking for what you need in front of a mirror in a clear, non-whiney voice

II. <u>The Complainer</u>

1. Figure out what you are feeling right now.
2. Write down if your basic needs have been met.
    -Are you hungry?
    -Are you tired?
    -Are you getting the attention that you need?
3. Practice saying what your feelings are to your favorite stuffed animal.

III. <u>The Arguer</u>

1. Take a time-out by yourself.
2. Figure out what the real problem is.
    -Are you just trying to be right?
    -What would happen if you admitted you could be wrong?
3. Jog in place for 60 seconds, do 20 push-ups, do 20 jumping jacks.
4. Play your favorite music and sing-along.

IV. The Fighter

1. Take 10 long, slow, deep breaths.
2. Go to your room and pet your favorite stuffed animal for 5 minutes.
3. Put on some music and dance.
4. Call a friend on the phone and talk about something you are both interested in.

V. The Tear-Drop Kid

1. Draw a picture of what you are upset about.
2. Give the characters in your picture voices and have them discuss the problem.
3. Think about a safe, happy place that you like to go to.
4. Lie on your bed and relax with quiet music playing.

VI. The Foot-Stomper

1. QUICK! Take a time-out by yourself.
2. What animal are you feeling like right now? Act out the animal!
3. Write down the reasons you are upset.
    -Is this really important to you?
    -Is this worth getting in trouble over?
    -Can you talk about this problem calmly?
4. Practice talking about your problem calmly in front of a mirror.

VII. The Run-Away Kid

1. STOP! Before you run too far, don't get yourself into danger.
2. Pull out your journal. Write a story about what made you want to run-away.
    -Are you not getting your own way?
    -What are you running away from?
    -Is it possible to talk about your problem with the people you are with?
    -What are you feeling right now?
3. Draw a picture of what shape you are feeling like and why.
4. Make believe your stuffed animal just ran away from you. How do you feel about it leaving? Have your animal tell you what the problem is and try to come up with a solution.

IMAGINE THAT!

This is a fantasy word game that helps you get a deeper understanding of your child's thoughts and feelings. Ask your child to relax, use his/her imagination and complete each sentence. Tell him/her there are no write or wrong answers, that this is a game. Write down the answer that your child gives you.

When I grow up_____

I love to _____

If I could change one thing about myself _____

My favorite animal is _____

Dogs are cool because _____

If I were brave, I would _____

When I am with my dad I feel _____

Children tease me when _____

The thing I love the most about myself is _____

Moms are _____

When I look at the sky _____

If I were rich _____

When I get big _____

If I had three wishes they would be _____

My best friend likes me because _____

I feel sad when _____

When I am bad _____

School makes me _____

I once dreamed _____

Rainbows are _____

I feel happy _____

Grandparents _____

When I am alone _____

Teachers are nice when _____

My friends get mad at me _____

If I could change one thing about my family _____

When I am sleeping _____

I feel nervous when _____

When I think about my mom _____

I really wish _____

Bugs are _____

I heard a story _____

I am proud _____

I hate getting punished because _____

When I look in the mirror _____

Mood Changer Tips For Kids

talk to a friend   do 25 jumping jacks   sing a song

   ride your bike   draw a picture of how you are feeling

        punch a pillow

write a story about what happened   ask a parent for advice   run in place for 2 minutes

        take 5 long slow deep breaths   scream into a pillow

                                            Brush your pet

        talk to a stuffed animal   soak in the bathtub with bubbles

                dance to the music

        Play your favorite song and sing-along

call your grandparent   help your mom cook dinner   stretch your muscles

        Meditate - pretend you are on the beach listening to the waves

use colors to show how you are feeling   take a nap   take a walk

     meditate - **imagine you are the king of your own universe**   blow bubbles

play with a friend   hit a bucket of golf balls   go for a swim

        talk to the person you are mad at - tell him how you are feeling

make a new friend   jump rope for 10 minutes   Draw cartoons

     write a poem   yell at yourself in front of the mirror   take your pet for a walk

write down 5 nice things about yourself

                        Write 5 nice things about the person you are mad at

ask your mom to massage your neck

            think about what happened - play it out with your stuffed animals

        SMILE – LAUGH

read a book   Laugh and Look in the mirror

                        Tell a joke

     tape record yourself laughing - Listen to your tape

                        Give yourself permission to have fun!

<u>Q</u>uality <u>U</u>nique <u>I</u>maginative <u>C</u>reativity for <u>K</u>ids
Q.U.I.C.K.

Parents: We know you have limited quality time to spend with your cuties. Children are always looking for attention whether negative or positive. In as little as 5 extra minutes you can give your kids some quality positive time.   Have fun and don't be afraid to use your imagination!

Give your child a neck and back massage.

Make up and sing a silly song together.

Start out a sentence with "once upon a time", take turns making up a story. End it with "the end".

Have your child draw a picture about the story you both made up.

Put on a fun song and dance together. Sing too if you want!

Take deep breaths and stretch.

Lay on the floor together and have a tickle contest.

Stare into each other's eyes and see who will laugh first.

Get out the lotion and give each other a hand massage.

Get on a three-way call with a grandparent or friend and tell them a joke.

Make up jokes. (Wouldn't it be funny if...?)

Play a game of cards (i.e., go fish, uno, war).

Make a bowl of jello. Have it for dessert!

Have a flower drawing contest.

Brush each other's hair.

Make up a poem about each other.

Play a game of checkers.

Make a salad for dinner.

Make funny faces...who can make the funniest face and laugh first.

Take your pet for a walk.

Have a bubble blowing contest.

See who could drink a cup of water the fastest.

Meditate. Imagine the two of you are dolphins swimming in the sea.

Play hide-and-seek.

Make a refreshing nutritious shake. (Use fruit, yogurt, ice-cream, milk, juice, ice)

Play a game of "Simon Says".

Read a book together.

Take silly pictures of each other.

Use flash cards to practice math or reading skills.

Laugh, Laugh, Laugh!

THIS CERTIFICATE IS PRESENTED TO

_____

ON THIS _____ DAY OF _____, 200___

FOR MASTERING THE ART

OF SELF-CONTROL

CONGRATULATIONS AND KEEP UP THE GOOD WORK: _____

About the Author

Pamela M. Goldberg is the "really cool" counselor in the Camp MakeBelieve stories. She is also the Founder and Director of the Camp MakeBelieve program. Pam has a private counseling practice in Las Vegas, Nevada, where she helps parents learn the skills necessary to raise their children with love, structure, and creativity. Ms. Goldberg has helped hundreds of children in her Camp MakeBelieve program learn to become better motivated, more relaxed, have better self-control and best of all to be happy. Happy kids talk to their parents about their problems and what is happening in their lives. Happy kids help out at home, do well in school and have friends. One of Pam's primary goals in dealing with parents is to erase the "mystery" of what goes on in child therapy. Through education and support, Pam assists parents in learning the skills necessary to not only help children express themselves better, but help parents deal with the information they receive. She wants parents to become the person their child seeks out when they need advice or support. Through reading and discussion of the stories in Become a Master of Self-Control with The Kids of Camp MakeBelieve, along with doing the workbook activities, both you and your child will have fun learning how to relate better to each other and to your environment.

Ms. Goldberg happily resides in Las Vegas with her supportive husband of 20 years. Together they have raised three adorable sons in a modern blended family. Pam probably understands kids so well because she was brought up in a dual-working household with 8 rambunctious brothers and 3 responsible sisters. Pam's parents are alive and well and very proud of their daughter's professional involvement with children.

About the Illustrator

Jimmy Boring is an art teacher in the fastest growing school district in the nation. When he is not busy introducing kids to the wonderful world of line, shape, color and texture, he draws his silly little cartoons for whoever will look at them. Mr. Boring is currently living happily ever after somewhere in Las Vegas.

About the Creative Assistant

Elizabeth Arthur (A.K.A. Liz) is a mother of three little darlings with a blended family making up a total of five children, all under the age of 13 years old. Liz has experience with children facing the problems of different behaviors...and knows exactly how it affects a family! An inspiring writer, mother and wife, Liz realizes the importance of taking control of your household, your health and well-being. She lives happily in Las Vegas with a very helpful and supportive husband who encourages her to be creative (along with giving her a great outlook on the family life!).